**TANURE OJAIDE** was born at Okpara Inland in the Delta area of Nigeria. He was educated in Nigeria, and received a B.A. in English from the University of Ibadan in 1971. He later gained an M.A. in Creative Writing (1979) and a Ph.D. in English (1981) from Syracuse University in the U.S.A. After teaching African Literature and Creative Writing for ten years at the University of Maiduguri, he spent the academic year of 1989–90 as visiting Johnston Professor of English at Whitman College, Walla Walla. He currently teaches at the University of North Carolina at Charlotte.

Ojaide is a Fellow in Writing of the University of Iowa; has been inducted into the Ahmadu Bello University Creative Writers' Club's Roll of Honour; and is a member of the Association of Nigerian Authors (ANA). He was Africa Regional Winner of the Commonwealth Poetry Prize in 1987; Winner of the All-Africa Okigbo Prize for Poetry in 1988; and also the 1988 Overall Winner of the BBC Arts and Africa Poetry Award. His publications include: *Children of Iroko* (1973), *Labyrinths of the Delta* (1986), *The Eagle's Vision* (1987), *The Endless Song* (1989), *The Fate of Vultures* (1990) and *The Poetry of Wole Soyinka*.

# TANURE OJAIDE

# THE BLOOD OF PEACE
## AND OTHER POEMS

**HEINEMANN**

Heinemann International Literature and Textbooks
a division of Heinemann Educational Books Ltd
Halley Court, Jordan Hill, Oxford OX2 8EJ

Heinemann Educational Books Inc
361 Hanover Street, Portsmouth, New Hampshire, 03801, USA

Heinemann Educational Books (Nigeria) Ltd
PMB 5205, Ibadan
Heinemann Kenya Ltd
Kijabe Street, PO Box 45314, Nairobi
Heinemann Educational Boleswa
PO Box 10103, Village Post Office, Gaborone, Botswana

LONDON   EDINBURGH   PARIS   MADRID
ATHENS   BOLOGNA   MELBOURNE
SYDNEY   AUCKLAND   SINGAPORE
TOKYO   HARARE

**Acknowledgements**
The poem 'No Longer Our Own Country' first appeared in
*London Magazine*; and the poem 'You Know Why' first appeared in
*The Syracuse University Magazine*

British Library Cataloguing in Publication Data
Ojaide, Tanure The blood of peace
I. Title
821
ISBN 0435 91193 7

PR
9387.9
.0373
B55
1991

Phototypeset by Wilmaset, Birkenhead Wirral
Printed and bound in Great Britain by
Cox and Wyman Ltd, Reading, Berkshire

91  92  93  94  10  9  8  7  6  5  4  3  2  1

# CONTENTS

# THE WARRIOR'S TRAIL

# VERDICTS

# Tunnels

Inside the priest graze the cows
he needs for sacrifice
to wipe off the communal scourge;
inside the hunter bark the hounds
tracking the prize game;
inside the drunkard live a tribe of bees
that do not sting when drenched.
And inside the singer flourish notes
for the songs
with which he steels himself
to tunnel through the dark
into a vast clearing.

# The Beginning of the Dream

We live in the direction of the wind
on whose back rainstorms ride;
we are forever blessed with fruitful possibilities.
The cropper mixes floods of sweat with the soil —
it is only with soiled hands that we can
build barriers against fireclouds of hunger.
We begin the dream in our wakefulness.

# The Bird in the Island

They have put a bird in an island,
and it dares not fly out.
Not for lack of an *iroko*[1] tree to perch on,
not for no allurements in a colourful world.

Unclear vision holds down the bird
that needs more light for flight –
dark clouds still cover the pilot's eyes,
bushes sprawl in the sky.

And the bird only flaps its wings
in anticipation of light,
set for the infinite, dreaded freedom.

[1]*iroko*   a very big and tall rain-forest tree, around which certain traditional rituals are performed

# As We Set Out

As we set out on this pilgrimage
fresh with memories of missteps,
let us be guided to the true god.
Many brought back gold, icons;
they brought back themselves, without
the second selves they went for;
they brought back respectable names
but no souls to match them.
Some went to serve themselves
and cannot now free their heads
from nets they wove in their prayers;
their homes are prison-houses.
Others fell sick upon kissing holy ground;
they returned, dead.
What are we praying for
with empty souls?
What can we invoke with loose tongues?
What do we look for
in a blindfold?
As we set out on this pilgrimage,
seeking a third chance
to live upright and die right,
let us be guided to the true god
of light and love.

# *Entering the Night*

Who does not know night, haunt
of marauders, coven of tyrants;
who does not know its hideous face?
Whatever lies therein is infernal:
missiles that are deadly,
beasts dying for preys,
clouds covering wandering spirits.
Who knows the explosives
enveloped in its silence?
In the security of its vast home,
night in a dark armour
sets its frightful ambush
and draws in casualties.
Who does not know that
night is a battle state?
Still, it's only those who don't dream
that will not venture into the night,
will not expose their bodies –
we must carry those fainting in our hands
across night to the infirmary of dawn,
we must answer the lover's call through night
with the warmth of our body presence.
What are bullet scratches
at the end of the battle
to salvage a generation
from the teeth of pain?

# Why Should We Not Die?

First came *rinderpest*[1].
The vegetarians in our midst didn't care
about the killer of cows.
Then came locusts and drought,
and the night fell upon all.
The people blamed it on the head,
the head blamed it on the people;
they didn't believe in shared responsibility.

The oracle says that our problem
will be solved in the long run.
Let it not be by the death of all.
There are no carriers yet for the sacrifice
and the people always blame the head,
the head always blames the people
for what either or both can bear with love.
Why should we not die of hunger?

---

[1]*rinderpest*   an acute, usually fatal, virus disease of animals such as
cattle or sheep

# No Longer Our Own Country

We have lost it,
the country we were born into.
We can now sing dirges
of that commonwealth of yesterday —
we live in a country
that is no longer our own.

Our sacred trees have been cut down
to make armchairs for the rich and titled;
our totem eagle, that bird of great heights,
has been shot at by thoughtless guardians.
Our borders have been broken loose
to surfeit the exotic appetite for freedom,
our flag ripped off by uncaring hands.
Counting the obscenities from every mouth,
the stupor, the deep wounds in our souls,
you can tell that we live in a country
that is no longer our own.

Where are the tall trees
that shielded us from the sun's spears,
where are they now that hot winds
blow parching sands
and bury us in dunes?
Where are those warriors
careful not to break taboos
who kept us from savage violations,
now that we face death?
Where are the healers
who offering themselves as ritual beasts
saved their neighbours from scourges?

We will expect in old age
to climb the mountain of prosperity
which we blew up in adolescence.
Our own country was a dream
so beautiful while it lasted,
and now we are exiles
in a country that was once ours –
we were born into another country,
a world that has gone
with a big boom.

But we will not perish in this other country.
We have lived through death
to this day,
we have deposed ourselves
and depend on alms that come our way.
We now know
what it is to lose our home,
what it is to lose a hospitable place
for this exile.
We expect the return of good days
and wiser, will no longer
let them pass from us.
For now we live in a country
that is no longer our own.

*3–5 October, 1986*

# All That Remains

*after visiting the National War Museum and 'Ojukwu's Bunker' at Umuahia*

All that remains:
a dishevelled, puddled cave
with a thousand mouldy rooms.

All that remains:
a crippled B52
surrounded by disabled tanks.

Now that we have returned from the jungle
with our souls still smarting from deep wounds,
we know what to wear before venturing again into the
                                                    wilds;

now that we have tasted blood and palm oil
and know which has turned us into brutes,
we will be wiser in our future choices.

After the plunge into great depths
to grope for salvation,
a sojourn in the bowels of the earth,
after flights down the unknown territory,

all that remains of that frenzy,
that riot of guns,
the delirium, the passion,
the stampede, the howls,
the bright blood,
the dream and the nightmare,
the truth and the falsehood,

only a silent cave, dark
and uncomfortable
and the bewildered eyes of a wanderer
glued to glossy pictures
without a guide.

*6 December, 1986*

# The Judgement of the Wanderer

Very soon those who cry for the tree to be downed
will weep that the cut is too deep –
'Are the cutters not wound-weary?'
Very soon those who want to rid the world of evil
will express shock at the execution of armed robbers –
'Have they no heads who commit this carnage?'

Very soon those who seek to silence others
will have to face the stone-heads of the graveyard
and run back to the barbed words of their critics,
very soon those who sue for peace with the hawk
will be firing missiles at the fugitive of justice,
very soon your strides will go beyond your lot
and you will be a violator of human rights.

> But to be mute is to be dead wood,
> to secure oneself is to be self-jailed,
> to turn back is to be routed
> and to stand still is to be dead alive.

Very soon the firebrands will be taking chameleon steps
on the ash-duned landscape of their brazen dreams;
very soon, very soon those who shut their mouths
not to hurt those who hurt the most
will throw the world around them into a nightmare
from which nobody wakes completely human.

# Verdicts

Let victors spit at the failed warrior's corpse,
others anoint it with *sosorobia*[1] –
the world curses the snake for its venomous nature;
in *Tivland*[2] they chant its praises day and night
for ferrying them across the great river to life.
And even if the ram dies bleating its rejection
of the priest's prayer to his own god, unheard
even if the judge, himself sentenced to life,
condemns the scapegoat to be slaughtered,
even if the patriot is hanged for treason,
let no verdicts be ever final –
the heart opens only to a secret conclave;
the rest of the world does not know the many paths
that public light cannot display.
So the majority curse and spit at whom
the initiate knows to be like them, not
everybody's favourite, not everybody's love.
Let victors spit at the failed warrior's corpse,
others anoint it with *sosorobia*.

*18 March, 1986*

[1]*sosorobia*    local perfume sold by Hausa traders
[2]*Tivland*    a part of Nigeria's middle belt and home of the Tiv people

14

# For W.S.

The Eagle has ascended.
The rocks of Idanre speed his wings.
No height is beyond him
who has kept the company of gods.
Now Ogun stands at the rockhill
overwhelming the sky,
his fruits a burst of colour.
Here is the long-sought harvest,
here the first species of unfettered growth
on the hard soil, broken loose
with scythes and hoes fashioned
in the smithery of Aké.
Let the Eagle's vision guide us,
let Ogun's spritely strides speed us
to the concourse of giants.

*16 October, 1986*

# The Prize

When you've won the prize
to which you consecrated your body
and soul, what happens?
Clear phlegm from the throat
and sing a victory song . . .

After a hunter stalked a wonder-game
for over half his years,
tore through the world
before downing it,
what drumming and singing will be enough
for his remaining days?

In victory, what fears
grip the celebrant who will now
be a different person,
no longer a hunter after the great kill
for which he must now disarm,
no longer the assailant
but the hostage of his own captive!

What will happen to his metal
after bagging the game for which
he honed it to the finest point?
If disabled by joy,
what will happen to his shield
against smiles, most deadly missiles;
what will happen to the firebrand
he brandished in the air
to earn his praise-name?

And will a bigger game chase him
from the security of victory,
will a wilder thing taunt him
from the communion of communions
to break the pact with his heart?

There are indistinct visions
that keep the victor half-sated,
half-haunted by his own prize.
What would I do with a dream game at dawn,
after the nightmare of blood?

*23 December, 1986*

# The Report

Back from the raid
into the wilds,
back from hidden battles
with wizards of foes,
back to the expectant
and searching communal eye

where is the elephant
I knocked down,
where the skulls of buffaloes,
hyenas and rhinos;
where the star fish I netted,
where the loot of victory?

Nobody asks about
the many trials in the bush,
nobody asks about
the eclipses and nights
before the sun sparked
the vision of power.

Despite the warrior's ready weapons,
he may yawn, spent from start
and unable to give the first
of seven blows . . .

O Song, may these amulets
dream-prepared and worn
invisibly in the heart
impress me with the wakefulness
of an astute guard.
And may these gifts of arms
fill me with the resolve
to head off the avalanche
of miseries daily threatening
with helpless death . . .

There are things to report,
things brought to a head
crying to be displayed
and trumpeted:
I have not caught the one game
that more than fills the bag,
none of the catch
that more than fills the fishing gourd.

Others who come back
wave certificates, wands
before the fratricidal war.
These people have streets and towns
bearing their coloured names;
womenfolk dance for these victors,
girls smile into their hearts
as drummers invent new notes
to praise strength and wealth
and megaphones blare their feats.

But gone and come back,
I am the witness
to the warrior's smothered cry,
tears dammed up in raw guts.
I am the witness
to uneven portions
that fill the field of possibilities.

I, who fly kites with scripts
whose interpreters
read only prejudices into lines;
I, who warm drummers
with the fire I keep blazing
with their drums
because they make heroes
of robbers and murderers;
I, the wind blowing away
the falcon's eggs
to end a dynasty of tyrants;

this, my only find:
one I cannot wave
to those waiting for me.
I display the fighting spirit
of the wandering soul,
unsubdued but not filled.

*14–17 June, 1986*

# The Fisherman's Dream

Rigs rose over me.
And ahead hell flared and fumed –
The chance god had invented his own sun, I thought.
It was all waters
as if there was no more land.
I paddled my plastic boat with fans.
The undertow was black miasma
vomited from cavernous mouths,
reeking of crude alcohol.
Hyacinths festooned my course.
I threw my net, perforated by flying sharks,
into the dark future of water
and it melted away.
The hooks I took along
held my clothes to weeds –
I succeeded in recovering myself
from the sewing needles of the hooks
and the nylon threads of the weeds.
And coming my way a flotilla of cadavers
with mourners in white overalls.
Wrapped in a stretcher, something
like the slim beauty of the mermaid.
'They've killed my love,' I howled.
And they came under cover of fish-planes.
In the confusion I wondered
whether I should turn back or go ahead.
I never can tell how I got home,
only to make love in a water-bed.

Then I went to buy fish
at the firing range turned market.
I didn't have a penny
to pay for a whale of a fish!

*Yaddo, 19 August, 1987*

# For Our Own Reasons

We have come out for our own reasons.
We cast fish-nets in the rain to exorcise famine,
we dispatch and receive messages through the wind,
and we want draughts of freedom in the open.
How can we live in the cave of obscurity
and still know the properties of light?
We wouldn't be hiding and seeking
if the world were not a haunted residence.

For us who have chosen to subdue the bull of life,
there's blood in the air and we are not scared –
the hermit imbibes the wisdom of the wilderness
from the wild cherries he lives on.
We are of one mind with the storm
to level the dead woods to give more light
to the evergreens.

What will we look up to without birds
beating their wings above our heads,
what will we look up to without trees
thrusting their arms into the sky,
what will we look up to without the crest of hills?
Our roots drive deep into the soil;
they sustain us in our search for fortune.

We shall return, carrying on our faces
either dazzling prizes or bruises of undeterred blows;
but we would have come out for our own reasons.

# Waking

Suddenly I wake from a nightmare
to the chorus of the wind and birds,
couriers singing songs of the earth.
The veil is falling off the face of the sky
and the sunflower that has been muffled
by a vast dark cloud, breathes visibly
and smiles openly a lovely aroma.
My eyes are dew-glazed.
If we can treat our deep wounds
in the clinics of night, if
the sea of sleep swallows our stream
of tears into its cavernous underbelly,
we will wake whole and strong.

After waking from the nightmare,
I shed tears
for the daybreak of Africa.

*9 February, 1987*

# On the Mountain

On the mountain of fortune, look
at the vast expanse ahead;
look at the landscape that has to be kept
now that you have accepted the gift
which must be made dearer
every year of the tenure.
Now that you are awake, see
the brigands that have taken over
and must be routed soon
to savour the cherries of freedom.
Now that you have ventured out, see
the swollen eyes still crying
to be provided for
from the cosmic abundance.
Now that you have washed, see
the land that needs to be scrubbed
with bare hands.
Now that you have got up, see
the world that must be awakened
with a loud drum . . .
Look at the millions to be healed
at the infirmary
not yet built in the land.
On this mountain of fortune, look
at the day ahead, spread out
with unbounded wealth
and sacrifice.

*10 March, 1987*

# The Rule of the Tortoise

Break up the shell of the tortoise.
Never satisfied, he eats and eats
and some day will eat our tripe.
Break up the wings of the vulture
that always hovers over our starved bodies,
lest his prayers be answered.

Break up the shell of the tortoise,
break up the wings of the vulture;
break them with hoes
forged in angry guts.
And beat up those singers
whose honey-laced tongues
have prolonged our pain.

Resist the rule of the tortoise
and the vultures will disperse
without a cannibal feast.

# Birds of Admiration

They evoke admiration
as they spread out over the sky.
None of them plucks from the other's plumes
to speed up its own flight;
none is *All-of-you*,
because there's no tortoise in their lifescape,
no unevenness in the sky they plough.
And they pull each other along,
devouring a whole region of distance
in their calibrated moves –
there's no cabal of flamboyant crooks
leaving behind the multitude
to a miserable state.

I would think serpents and scorpions
sprout in human heads
to keep others down, disabled
to make it easy to rob unchallenged.
And cheetahs and dogs are so fast
to keep others eternally behind.
Your beauty is my ugliness,
your lightness my darkness,
your victory my woeful defeat
and your mountain of prominence,
the lowliness of the commonwealth.

Don't tell me you aren't mean,
you rival of a man!
But these birds evoke my admiration
as they spread out evenly over the sky.

# Before Our God

Neither bullets nor other savageries can arrest words
that have already been aired –
paper is witness to the lone mind.
Visible, this length of beard sprawling outside the house;
visible, this smoke whose fire is fuelled in the heart;
vibrant, this drum that cannot be drowned by thunder.
These words file out on the dirt road
to stop nerve-wrecking waves of despots;
they are the charms worn before battle.

> Missiles are like burrs on fowls,
> they fall off;
> curses are pebbles on the dog's back,
> they fall off.

Neither bullets nor other savageries can arrest these words
that I have already aired.
Paper is witness to the lone mind.

# THE
# BLOOD
## OF
# PEACE

# I

## FLOODGATES

## *Invocation*

Birds entertaining the sky with melodies
add your voice
to my anthem of communion

Trees buttressed in the earth's bosom
give depth
to the crier's questing voice

Hurricanes of the storm season
sweep from everywhere
a labyrinth of notes

for again I must sing.

Pools gathering in a deluge
into a full stream
lend currency to my song

Moon, full to the brim of night,
you owe my tongue
a mirror of brilliance

Feathers of my singing creed
fly me to an unassailable pitch
in the songscape ahead

for I must sing
rainsong to fructify the desert
fishsong to revive dying streams
harvestsong to fill the body
matingsong to multiply lovers
warsong to arm the threatened

And if this voice must be heard
above the tinsel prattle of slick tongues,
if this cry must register whole
in the mindscape of men,
O mentors and masters,
weave me the utterance
to foil the fiercest face;
let my words bristle, a beehive
with honey and stings
to dispense
according to the season's needs

for again I must sing
and I sing the endless lifesong
with tutored lips . . .

# Ancestral Saliva

I
On every tongue fire
that flares to be slaked;
on every lip silence
that cries to be broken.

And I will follow the dirt road of roots
to the subterranean sea,
follow the camel through frontiers
to desert water-holes.
I want to be filled, a mountain
with streams.

The wind thirsts for distances,
the eye thirsts for visions,
the hand thirsts for blows,
the head thirsts for heights,
I thirst for rivers
whose silts crop barns.

In our thirst
the winds beat us with gusts of expectation.
Beyond the horizon, flashes
of fruited longing;
in the silence of advancing days
clouds shower gifts
at austere faces.

II

When the sun exhales fire
to smite faces,
there's acute thirst
only another season
can assuage.

The fowl's blood sputters
for the sky to blush black
and the duct breaks loose
upon the stretched body
of the panting earth.

    Obliterate
    dust with water,
    obliterate
    hunger with manna

And the hoe bruises the earth's
flesh, fending for love;
the tractor bites
with its spade tooth
to open up the heart
for a harvest of festivities.

And each of the million droplets
kindles memory
with kid's play songs
and a farm of rituals
that sprout climbers
of crops.

My tongue is touched
with ancestral saliva
and I shall sing
the perennial song
of seasons

Life out of ravages,
fruits out of sweat,
blessing of tears.

And now beyond the horizon
a storm brews.
Along this road
hurricanes will strew
my life
with fluting reeds . . .

## II

**FLUCTUATIONS**

# *In the Hills*

In the hills
the winds mutter to the accompaniment of echoes
the tigers of rage
they unleashed at the plains.

And because neighbours hauled in their grains
before this banditry
of the flying horses of the cosmos,
they laugh at my vacant home.
Their laughter only relieves me.

The earth, foliaged green
with gratitude for lifeblood,
is altar to the sky.
And where else than in between
can there be the parade of pain,
where else than the den
will the tiger lie low?

Gong-salute to the wild winds
that bring the wanderer home
to the virtue of nativity,
tongue-salute to wind-guts!
My tongue, loosen up your roots
to lash at idols
who curse the hands
that mould them for worship.

Let me be a palm
root to crown
in the perennial season
of strong winds.

# When the Shuttle Bird Sings

When the shuttle bird sings,
time's at a standstill
and memory is rife with experiences
of future pains.

When the shuttle bird sings
of its plumage of gold,
there's a hailstorm
and a shadow savages its beauty
with a stream of blood —

no one comes this far
without a taint of the flood
fresh with the red
of youths, a game of flesh
in the ritual strangers sought
with a cool eye for pearls.

Next door to today
squats the owl
now a soothsayer
after the door closed on it
the vision of beauty —
its hooting, smile or cry,
echoes the same fright.

Whatever one season takes away,
another replenishes —
I sing of loss and recuperation.
And the bird of fate
forever shuttles
with the gold of ages
to dazzle today's glum faces . . .

# Nubile Girls

In the market nubile girls
break their hearts for strangers . . .

Separated in a hard way,
now rehabilitated on high heels,
I see them in *Leventis* and *Kingsway*[1]
wraiths of dead pubescence
dressed for the supermarket.

The birds of yesterday
have changed climate
for more colour to their plumes.

But who will gather flowers
strewn by djinns in the air,
who will covet the stranger's disease?

[1]*Leventis* and *Kingsway* expatriate department stores in Nigeria,
where expensive luxury items are sold

# Moon Phase

At night we ran out
to fetch the moon,
our bowl a net of laughter

> When a lion
> the delta is my den
> the desert my haunt

We never knew in the hunt
that the elephant was a musician,
a tusk of rhythm

> When a rock
> the sky is my crown
> a cloud of granite

We never knew
the snake would make skin merchants
without a bite

> In water
> the shark polices
> the dominion of scales

And those who phased their lives
in backlogs of tides
glaze themselves in readiness
for swipes of cotton

Till today the *obeche*[1] wood remains
door to our vacant thoughts.

[1] *obeche*  tropical hardwood found in the rain-forest area of West
Africa; used in making furniture

# Desert Kiss

(Written after a sandstorm which blacked out day in
Maiduguri for about forty minutes in June 1988)

The sun blazed the morning
with crystal shots;
the lines fluttered cotton
aired to throw away dank smell.
There was nothing in the swallow's swoop
to turn back the heels,
nothing in the faces of others
to dismiss the day.

And in the first real kiss of the desert,
the Sahel was blind to public rebuke.
Couldn't tell clouds blackening
with rage, smoke from heavens
perforated with shuttle rockets;
mountains ranged fire
and in the distance the apocalypse
on magic heels, a savage sweep.

Memory lost itself in alleys
probing for precedents, none
for age to boast of
'before your birth'.
The desert's clear message to the forest,
a new cheek of the cosmos
fouled with distant dust.
Surprise, the soul of accidents,
leaves no room for manoeuvres.

There's comfort in dusk –
the ambush of light is taut,
the armour of night is fright.
I have started to feel the fluff of thorns,
too late to make a bed of briars
in the tall bush.

They ask the nomad to go home,
but to what home in a dune of dream;
to what home
in an oasis in the skyline?

# At the Confluence

*for Joe Ewubare, after the accident*

Within the clearing of light,
broad-faced winks
and colour-loud flashes . . .

When the ambush is done
and fate assured of its craft,
all winds blow the victim
off his plotted way –
his guards lose their eyes and watch,
granite habits fragment
and warrior-charms are foiled
in the lightning of encounter.

And then a smog of vision,
a bang of nothing. Nothing
and a hulk of flesh, breathless . . .

What can even Aridon retrieve
from the divine vault
when squeezed from metal ruins
with snapped ribs and cannibal cuts?
What can be recalled till days after
white-masked, gloved attendants
drained the outer heart of blood
and family and friends drowned
suns and moons in deep streams?

The day keeps a blind agenda
on its palm of light,
the vision of terror is lost in clouds
when the ambush tantalises with speed –
no hours behind, no days ahead
the confluence of roads
the winds blow in a sure catch
into a crash of wheels.

And life freewheels on rubber,
freewheels on metal,
macadam, laterite,
on all fours
with circus perils . . .

## Our Seasons

Seasons bring to life old memories –
always in their company, young and old
and when we have not counted the survivors
from one assault, fresh eye-snares
blind us to reflection.
They never surrender their mystery
to predictions of schooled seers.

Tireless workers, the seasons
give birth to ants, plasterers
who restore beauty to cracked bodies;
they give birth to winds, prompters
whose breaths keep generations on strong feet;
they bring in strange birds
whose feathers are magic shields.

And the seasons tend the land
with a yearful of hands.
They spring out rainbows
to cross deserts of days,
they blow a bevy of flints at webs
that lie in ambush of hope;
their fires burn briars of hate
and their winds always carry the song
over dunes to enrich the echoes.

Water is friend and foe,
the problem spouse
impossible to live without.
And the sun tests his missiles
with the wickedness of a wayward father
before blessing the strong as his children
with dawn, opening to light.

And many are the gifts of seasons:
the obsidian armour of light,
the crystal shield of darkness,
the pollen of beauty,
the dew of restoration
and the cycle that leaves man as man.

In the beginning, they say,
God hid in every river and hill
to show his ways to fishes and hunters.
Today he is lost in the fog
that smothers the sun
and ruins the sea
with the blood of the moon.

O seasons, you are death and birth,
debt and strength, the perennial
flood that will not drown us
in spite of our clay selves.

# Recession

A wilderness recedes
into a garden of *eggplants*[1]
in my palm.

The winds, couriers of gods,
will not pay back gossips
with closed lips.
'No amendment to natural laws,'
taught the sick sage.
Only roots sprouting upwards
startle the sky with deformities.

And the sea will carry the blues
of my tears;
when next it rains,
look out for remains of salt,
dust showers.

Leave to scales fish flavour,
leave barks a tenement of trees;
destiny's clasped to the skin
and that's the bane of borrowing,
picking holes to breathe through.

When the locust tribe arrives
consuming legumes and greens,
celebrate the dearth
with their brittle bodies –
so fragile, destroyers.

In the season's pouch,
such familiar stuff
and a flock of surprises.
Hence the wilderness recedes
into a garden of eggplants
in my bruised palm.

---

[1]*eggplants*    aubergines

# Remembrances

Remembrances of hallmarks,
towers from where the sky-god calls out
and rings ritual bells of awe, applauds
the tick-feat, an elephant-lift of teeth.

There are echoes clearer than the voice,
voices with the report of thunder
from wherever you hear them
they smoke through the pale of childhood;
they beat chamber-doors with insistence:
'You cannot leave me to your sleeves.'

In the backward flight
across dead seasons of blue years
you'll trip over mountains.
Remembrances of busy streams of night,
remembrances of stone carriages
across creeks of laughter,
hollow weeks when the palm blisters
with the triumph of a banana peel.

Remembrances of mounds
the ants' throne
dissolved without salt
into forthcoming storms.
What generous game has been lost
to cluttered tracks!

And since forgotten tongues
leave no after-taste of love,
dig deep into cashiered records;
break through shadows
for a grip of fate.
In the face of wisdom flourish scars
of defeated diseases . . .

Remembrances of rainbow regions
where every day is smile-soaked,
a skyline of painted constrictors.
Remembrances of the ambush nobody escapes,
remembrances of fresh cries, sighs —
there's a cry from a mound,
the sort that revives the land.

What sieve can save me
from this flooded memory?

## Waves

I
With record fury
they inflict waves
of high wails
upon the land.

No luck with them,
warrior or peace gods
and their liveried force
prowling bloodstreams
to toast power.

Do not look to gods
who relish worshippers'
tearful faces, there's
no charity in their grace;
they relocate to escape
the fire of curses.

Do not call the police
to make arrests;
*kola-nut*[1] addicts,
they are caught up
in counters with piles
of unattended files.

And with record fury
they inflict waves
of high wails
upon the land.

II
These are the waves
we must ride through:
hills of sharks,
monster-heroes
capped with lust;
in their faces
severity.

These are the waves
we must ride
to the island
fraught with freedom.

And the waves
are wails of youths
with no grounds
to break,
the salt rock
we have to fly
through the blues.

And these are the waves
we must ride through . . .

¹kola-nut   the nut of the *Kola* tree. Common in the rain-forest area of
West Africa

# When My God Asks for a Song

Uhaghwa[1] has woken me
in the jungle of night,
asking for a song.
I offer the bee-song.

Bees of rage seek to burn
cheeks of chiefs whose stools
hide executive loot;
they swarm to tear off masks
of torturers whose face-swathes
endear them to their victims;
they charge at slavers
from all regions of rape.

And they will not sheathe their weapons
till the land's cleansed
of its omnipresent muck;
they will not stop the charge
with the wails of counterfeiters;
they will not stay the assault
until the triumph of dawn
over the vast army of night.
Truth will be the end,
death and birth.

Mine is the vision of stings
and honey, the dream of industry;
mine the memory of the truth
of pain. Out of fire
will come the hands
to revive the land.

[1]Uhaghwa   the god of songs among the Urhobo people of Nigeria's
Delta area

# The Testament

Upon every rare gem
a mediocre hulk
to foil the lustre,
the sun buried in black.

The seasons of my land
provide delight in dirges –
the dead are savaged flowers;
two bands of survivors:
the beleaguered tribe of stragglers
too erect for these crooked lanes
and the waves of beasts
masked with the skin of humanity.

I fear the ants will die
of firestroke, an ambush,
and only stunted hills will bear
their burnt banner of industry.

As frontiers collapse in the stampede
from the smarting hole,
do state chiefs hear the jest outside,
spite for the family of dwarfs
they raise with mean genes?

There are branches for every monkey,
and there's no end
to anyone's reach in the forest.
The eagle doesn't usurp the kite's perch.
O Earth, you are witness.

# Night Storm

Season of storms,
and cannons wrest me
from bed to flight
of fugitive winds
and flashes of divine flints.

O wind, you are lord here.
See the livery of leaves
shaking before you
and the clan of branches
bowing to you.
What majestic airs do you put on
that you are so adored?

Lightning, God's torch,
you show the way
to wanderers
through the jungle of night;
often you have given away
thieves from the dark,
registered restitution as your mission.
Your bolt will remain whetstone
to my voice.

Frogs sing themselves hoarse,
celebrating wealth of waters.
Everywhere flowing sheets
from the sky
to cover the earth's broad face.

The sun is drowned in black smoke,
the moon gone under the river
for a face-lift;
the earth lies belly-up
relieved of thirst, aflush
with cheerful tears.

Again, the stampede.
The wind must be wrestling
with waves on the sea-bed;
there's no surrender
to the dictates of desire –
the victor powers the night
with denial of vision.

Again, the fire.
This night's not for fireflies
to flirt with light,
not for damsels to dance
to the wild desires of body-rhythm –
the storm has eroded
the stars, and there are no paths
through the night.

There are further storms
fathomed in the land,
cannibal winds battening the heart
to give up
its stubborn hold to the earth's
drenched bosom,
bigger fires flaring up
the dark armour of robbers.

O season of storms,
I salute your potent presence
with this song
afloat in my deluged tongue.

# The Island

Before its discovery
by some sorcerer-at-arms
    a flower in the forest of waters,
    a sea-lit star,
    a genius hand's tapestry
    and a mascot of virginity.

Nobody's cultic throne;
footstool to none,
the island piety invites
with a welcome smile.

Then came one
with the head of a hyena.
He needed a voodoo grove
to invoke power over powers,
needed blood for a full term,
blood that would not smell
into open corridors.

A shooting range where
stealth guns are blood-proud,
the soil takes no bodies
but feeds the sea.
Bodies strapped to stone
discharged from copters
tell a dumb tale
of the triumph of warrior-kings.

The chilling air
and the ghosts of victims
are not the vacation robes
of islands.
And what waters around here
can wash away the stink
of the head and hands?

I have lost much of the tribe
whose song for change
I picked from the island.
In place of coconut palms,
water hyacinths.
I know why.
When generals triumph,
their guns are hardly heard.

# The Task of Hunters

The elephant, self-proclaimed king,
stomps the land with rock-feet;
every step grave, every measure
torture, a trail of tears.

Hunters fan out, beating their chests:
'Wherever the ravager reaches,
he will bite steel.'
But the magnate of power
has more than a thousand eyes
in one hard-boiled head,
his earphones more than cover the land;
missiles from nowhere strike down
whoever acknowledges the praise-name of hunter.

He has jumped over holes
grass-rugged to seat a throne of woes,
he has smiled out of every dance
billed to be led by death,
cut every day of judgement
and cleared away irritants with offerings.
Instinct has swelled his fate
with jinxed rivals,
years of war-trade have dressed him
with an armour of cunning.

To everyone seasons of smiles
and doomed affront.
And there are baskets of eggs
in the steel closet
to break the stubborn spell,
turn the sorcerer-king's stool
into a capsized boat.

The elephant still stomps the land
with rock-feet,
there are wails from his draconian steps,
grave-littered measures of rule.
Let hunters prepare themselves.

# The Blood of Peace

What I learnt by rote
I planted on a dry bed.

I could count verses
in pre-exam dreams of school days.
I could rifle through beads
without stopping anywhere
to ask them to talk back to me.

What did I know of the warsong
I chanted from the womb
before I bled from insecurity,
what did I know of passion
before I was shunned by whom I loved?
What I mouthed
did not catch the blaze
of my veins.

I learnt by rote the proud anthem
before the land wounded me.
The lion must have become
warrior-king of the jungle
many lives after dying of weakness.
The blood of peace stirs me into war.

What I planted by rote
sprawls all over
and stifles the landmass;
what I sang by rote
stays by grace of age.

When it storms, it floods here
and roots out the barns of rote.
I know why
the dog-bark dies in the street
without a back-turn.

# Worksong

It's from the ants,
the soldiering tribe,
that I learn my worksong.
It's from landmarks
of uncountable minorities,
the millennial triumph
of small things
that I draw my worksong.
It's with the grit
of their invisible teeth
that they cut high marks.
Every hand up,
the trail runs forward
with each carriage
into a mountain
that belittles loud mouths.
From sweat-enhanced genes,
from the chronicle
of proud colonies
I pick notes
for my worksong.
Their days always heave
with produce.
It's from the ants,
soldiering masons,
that I learn my worksong.

# For Whom Songs Are Made

We are herding on the flock
for the shepherd
to green grass
in the lion's haunt.

There's no song for sunbirds
chattering on low bushes,
only for the eagle lounging
on the *iroko*[1] top;
no song for journeymen who carry on
while the boss slumbers.

When the story is told of Gizeh,
Akhnaton supplants the million hands
that built faith on stones.
Who built the boats of Nana's fame,
who dug the moats that sealed off Benin?

Not one name is remembered
of slaves.

And we are herding on the flock
for the shepherd
to green grass
in the lion's haunt.

---

[1]*iroko*  a very big and tall rain-forest tree, around which certain traditional rituals are performed

# The Missionary

With no voice to cry out
its roles, the crab bears
the abuse of benefactors.
No place in the body to call head,
the teeth porcelain stumps planted in flesh;
the crab only sells an exotic dish.

It trails light prints of scissors
in its mission of holes.
Wherever there are survivors of drought,
homage to the unsung craft of the crab:
with its teeth it chisels the earth
into a hell of eternal waters.
I have made out-of-season catches,
profited from the spited industry
when the creeks lent out their draughts.

Once I believed fishes fell from the sky
in delta hurricanes.
I didn't know crabs abandoned holes,
bunkers for others
who came out of deluged abodes
wildly free as if from long-sentence jails
only to be caught in the vigilante nets
of fishers of boys.

My new faith is coloured with age,
a crab-gift of mysteries.
And there's no voice to cry out
against the abuse of benefactors.

# Another Company

Today my company's of another kind.
I slip into the dark
to invoke light
alone, alone.
I leave family and friends
for combat;
let me be lighter, stronger.
The forest's my company
with its bees, beasts,
daemons and flickers of sorcery.
Let me for once take
a hundred steps alone.

The hunter bears the night
alone, flares it with shots;
alone the wilderness
that's the soul
burning for salvation.
Alone today I devour the fright of night.
Yonder's lit with bonfires.
Just one finger
has to step out
alone in the cold
for others to see far.

And today I invoke ancestral hunters
of the lonely trail
to blaze the black night
with daring feet and hands.

# Headgears of Assailants

They have erected a wall
before the sea
to shut me off from the ever-blue prosperity
of mermaids;
they taunt my vision
to belittle me.

You will be record-lucky
to read the lines of your palms
in the fray of life,
you can be hauled
into the current
to carry away the stink of lords.
Even you who swear
not to give up the club
that's the fist
without a death-blow!

I hear ballads
of monsters tamed
by the egg of a fly.
How many see the sea
or sail in glorious ships
to the mountain resorts of beauty?

When the sun in its brazen love
commands a flock of migrant birds
to lie low,
another season begins.
I am boring
through the wall a line of blue
for a minute egg
to tame the waves and the winds,
headgears of assailants!

## Accomplice Sea

Again the sea, serene
accomplice of masqueraders,
rubbed salt on a savage bite.

On hunched backs, tripping
the waves bore them
shiploads upon shiploads
grey with bile-syrupy wastes.
Drums of death
in the same hold
where past centuries had stocked away
the tribe's strength.

After champagne-libating
their church-rifled land,
the crew straightened their nose
southwards, to where
old brutes, old allies
mindful of profit of hats,
beads and madras
would open their arms,
hearts and heads
to lucrative affront.

With relics of slaving shame,
helms and paddles of old craft
still on display
in the water-front,
Koko slept the last piece
of peace
the eve of the call.
In the dark, a witch-dance
the port a white coven
swept by black hands.

Again blinding gold
offered poor chiefs
to open up jungle estuaries.
The witches came to berth
at bedtime;
they found dogs of guards
hungry to the last.
They knew what titbits
would stop them from barking;
they overdosed them
with toxic sops, mint-flavoured
to be fool enough
to collaborate.

And when it came
for the ships to discharge
drums upon drums, sealed
with forged approval,
the constipating hands
stockpiled the forest
with poisons only white witches
can decontaminate.
And none outside their company
knew of the diabolic bond;
no red flag on the mast
to give up the mission,
the crew wore pious masks
of distant merchants.

While the green coat
slipped off evergreens,
villagers caroused
with unfamiliar draughts;
while everywhere was hotter
than a hellish hearth,
nobody at home cried foul
in the miscarriages of mothers;
nobody at home asked why
babies turned oldies
in the crib.

And the whistle
came from travelled sons,
true envoys of the tribe.
I salute guts
in a sea of prejudice.
After the whistle
blew sleep out of riverine eyes,
after creeks of rain
washed off scales of indifference,
the dogs and their pep racers
swallowed their vomit,
routed by rage of right.

When I look at the rich,
northern in the vane,
I see mean hands,
callous smiles.
And again the sea,
serene accomplice of masqueraders,
rubbed salt on the savage bite.

# Interlude: A Song

Whose brooms are most thorough
what shall he earn?

Whose brooms are most thorough
what shall he earn?

He sweeps away mountains
to rid everywhere of muck

He abandons not the lion's den
to the fate of victims

Whose brooms are most thorough
what shall he earn?

Whose brooms are most thorough
what shall he earn?

Favourite of the land
Giver of a proud face-lift

He deserves a hundred million hands.

# IV

## MOON PASSION, LOVE TIDES

### *Beautiful One*

I will give you your due
Beautiful One

Flowers have dazed me with their spell
but none with the magic strength
and fragrance of your presence

O Bride I sing
of the tended moon-face
with mirrors of smoothness

I have seen stars in the face of night
but not this vision
from a world that breeds no uneven contours

I know the unknown goddess
in her human incarnation
to take up a body-gift

I look up to you
with a hunter's prayer for a prize-game
the night's worth the day

Beautiful One
I will give you your very due.

## Her Fairness

I count days ahead
to the fair queen
by hallmarks of stone.
Wherever she presents herself,
gold to her glory.

And I must provide venison
for the royal feast,
I must wash her feet
with a wild bull's blood
to keep my place in front
of the invisible line.

I know from her heart
kernel juice,
hallucinating draughts;
there's tango in the cup —
what better brew
is balm to my afflicted soul?

I must carry the mirror
of the moon at her roundest
through the day,
and I sing of communion
and after-banquet grace:

she's very fair.

## Song Boat

I am sailing in a moonboat
at songspeed
I am heading for windfalls
that pave the way with flower stalks

Hasten after the hare
    there's no lair in the trail
run after the rat
    there's no hole to halt the race

And a word of grace, a sun-smile
after bidding time . . .

I am floating in a sea of winds
entranced in a love-grove
supplicant and beneficiary
at the secret altar of faith

Amble after the antelope
lest she be transfigured into a rock.

# When the Moon Filled the Void

My desire rose, a big void.
I was afraid of the vastness:
how can I fare well in the wilderness
with the webbed feet of the delta?

The earth became a grass-widow
and thirst turned me
into a nomad at heart;
the tongue shot out fire,
but there was no rain.

Fear created its own fortress
in nightfolds of armour –
with stone impulse
I waited on my trials
to spend themselves.

And suddenly lifted
from the dungeon of stupor,
I came to what I sought:
the moon sailed in
from a blue sea at rest.

# Love Song

The moon will be told of her beauty
under which we hide and seek our fill

Princess of Okene, there is balm
in every pore of your soul
Ebira Antelope, there is sleekness
in every step of your goal

The moon will be told of her beauty
under which we hide and seek our fill

Desert Captive, there is gold
to every soil you grace with your touch
Goddess of a new world, there is faith
in the songs of your worship

The moon will be told of her beauty
under which we hide and seek our fill

Spice of every day
Dancer inspiring the drummer
Song raising the voice of the singer
Gift of a lifetime

The moon will be told of her beauty
under which we hide and seek our fill

Your name is like your body
it evokes persistent freshness
I mutter the magic sound
for a vision of your full phase

The moon will be told of her beauty
under which we hide and seek our fill

Hunt of the Antelope takes me unscathed through briars
Sacrifice to the Princess opens me her bosom
Love of the Mermaid drives me to the sea of fortune
Worship of the Goddess transports me to the sky

The moon knows her duty
and we no longer hide to seek.

*29 May, 1988*

## 'I Warned You'

'I warned you' came
with laughter of hyenas.
I was transfixed with shame,
my heart a big stone
that pulled me down.
I was hostage of slaves.

And where is the vengeance of the storm
I was born with
now that I want to tear off
branches and roots
the fortress of those who mock me?
Where do they sheathe their teeth
that they are sharper than ever?

I need not tell them witches
that the moon is my favourite bird
perched in heaven,
her face pearl of the cosmos.
Whoever takes off for the tryst
incarnates an astronaut's soul
to reach the crown of grace.
But let him plan for a soft-landing back!

And the hyenas, slaves to laughter,
rally themselves. I am the island
assaulted by vicious waves.
They will never understand my love,
and they mock me hilariously with
'I warned you'.

# A Blind Day

The clearing of light bristles
with the pulse of a tigress.
Do not doubt the net of linen,
a web of rays;
you can hang
by the pitch beauty of locks.
Do not carry into your head
the stone myth of the mountain;
I have seen a mountain in flames.
Pass by the convent of uniform –
beneath, breasts pointing
feverishly to the heart.
Stone on fire,
a grass couch caught
in the flare of flint.
Shattered: a web of virtues,
titles to pass the day
with accolades of honour.
Who dares point fingers
of cowardice
at the tiger and his mate?
The clearing of light bristles
with the pulse of a tigress;
a blind day
in the full moon.

# A Song: For Festus Iyayi

*To ze-e*
*To ze-e*

The sacred ram that roamed the whole place
everybody knew it

*To ze-e*

The Oba's first son knocked it down
and reported I did the awful thing

*To ze-e*

I told them who did it
but they closed their ears

*To ze-e*

I tried to defend myself
but they shut my mouth with shouts

*To ze-e*

Very soon they will tie me down
and slaughter me with a ritual blade

*To ze-e*

May the Invisible Father protect
the parentless child of the land

*To ze-e*
*To ze-e*

V

**WATER FRUITS**

## *In the Cult of Water*

Generous winds blow the generous
into generosity;
the current accelerates a flotilla
of fishes, gourds of gifts.
Who meets the rivermaid
lives to tell a windfall tale . . .

The rain falls
upon a sweating body,
and who prays for more?
Couldn't have gone farther
than the river
to fish for beauty.

• • •

Turtles have no rattles:
they impress folklore
with their character.
The slow-paced are fast-witted,
their victory lasts, uncontested.

• • •

When the pond's stripped
of its swathe of water,
the only shelter is a mire –
out of the mud, fish
for a favourite dish.

• • •

From underwater
patience catches a snail
to fill its desire.
My teacher holds on till dusk
for a flounder;
a carp covers my face
with a fish-smile.

• • •

Worms seek the soft side
of the soil –
they are safe
until fishers tear the earth
for a bait.
Why do we not eat worms
that fish feed on?

• • •

Record rains replenish sun-
ravaged years –
the wolves of the sky
full to the clouds
weep crystal droplets;
their sorrow is joy:
children play in puddles,
plants smell good.

• • •

At Uzere, Eni[1] taunts me
with waters of judgement.
If I move slowly, it'll be said
I am half-dead with guilt
before trial;
and should I walk fast,
it'll be that Eni foreknows victims
before they are accused.
Free or not,
I am the perpetual suspect
and Eni taunts me
with clear but deep waters
of judgement.

. . .

Let's build a vast ship
to fill the water's breadth
and berth for all tribes
to board!
Is it for sovereignty
that armies with beastly heads
swarm both banks and aim rifles
at each other's heart?
Is it for freedom
that governments breed sharks
as if the bite of the economy
isn't savage enough?
The river is my tryst
and in it I make love to all peoples . . .

[1]*Eni*    an Isoko river-god famous in ancient times for detecting witches

# The Oracle of Dawn

The cock, chief oracle
in the sun-cult of dreams,
cries out for rituals of dusk
at crossroads.
Thereafter dark shutters
blinding horizons
burn off in sunflames.

The dew-drenched voice rebounds
with new life;
there will be a tryst
with day, a flood of light.
And ahead, spilt colours
that impress the earth with beauty –
faces once wrapped around, now erect
in the current of fashion.

Salute to the oracle
with his healing cry,
salute to the ever-open eyes
of the great dreamer!
For the bite of his words
(a harsh prescription for the plagued),
he may be martyred;
but his voice persists
with flight of fears . . .

It's hurricanes of songs,
cannons and downpours.
The rubbles of revolution
can always be swept away
after the thunder!

# Correspondence: From Home

*for Hyeladzira Balami*

It took a rock of time
and as you feared
Jos wanted me to stop for good
for a plateau of vacation
in Nok-old caves.
Luscious were the baits,
but they couldn't arrest me
and I arrived home, whole.

I have not come home
to retrieve the wealth
of halfpennies and cowries,
though jewels of antiquity
shine again
with the radiance of
a harvest sun.

I have come home
to revisit the tangles
of the land's tresses,
come to my first love
in her attire of green,
princess of charm
in the lush season of rains.

I will count one hour's pleasure,
only one hour of homely vision
that will not escape
with my restless feet
to other worlds;
I will recall the hour
on the soil
that enhances my voice
with the freedom of nativity.

Before me:
yam tendrils climb without arms
to yield barns
despite that army of beetles.
And when the priest sits before the shrine,
he doles out yam,
favourite of the living and the dead.

Plantain, rain-shield
of my infant days,
benefiting from backyard leftovers;
*kpekere*[1] crunches every minute
into a sweet experience
and *dodo*[2] makes beans and rice
a full dish.

Cassava is grace of mothers
and I keep goats
from its leaves of luxuriance.
From here starch goes to the rest
of the world, trades
for sea fish from neighbours
and farina is daily snack.
Of course, *garri*[3] is the belly's
staple medicine against hunger.

Rubber has revived my family
in harsh days –
was *Onoharigho*[4] mad
to plant trees about?
Okpara folks didn't know
the man of Burma fame
foreknew the value of money
in seeding trees
and never insulted its seekers.

Palms tower, aloft heads;
thatched homes are gone
but the king is always king;
the cork-tree, theme of songs
with *Odjoboro's*[5] craft so cheap of wood
but with which I drift
with dawn currents;
the *akata*[6] stick, the catapult
with which my half-blind father
shot down a hawk.

Up there the woodpecker,
jungle carpenter, forever working
on its parents' coffins
despite the fat boil in its mouth;
and there the parrot, chronicler
that speaks every language –
do I talk more because
when my mother was pregnant with me,
she drank medicine
done with its feathers?

I have come home
to the anthills
where the ant wears a crown
despite demons of giants
roaming the land.
I have trailed the porcupine
and borrowed its shafts
to arrest intrusion;
I take the antelope into my arms
for a love with divine fragrance –
it's forbidden to kill beauty
for the lust of a day.

I have come to the creeks
of the delta, come
to wash off dust;
come to dip into depths
and come out groomed
by water powers,
I have come to the streams
that fill my body
with life:

the Omwe with the big
and small sheets my haunt;
the Omoja full.
The hooks I lost
and the water I waded
still carry my touch
in its dark flood.

In these waters
the carp I better catch
than return, unrewarded
by the day;
the *oware*[7] jumps across the road,
the *ovworo*[8] tugs me,
the eel slips through my fingers,
the snake-fish – should I
burn my fingers
to roast a tasteless catch?
And the mud-fish before the cone net
means so much now –
I saw sex without knowing.

I have come home
to the greenery,
come home
to the equilibrium of land and water,
beautiful body of earth
with a delta of marks.
I have come home,
I have come home
I have come home.

*Okurekpo & Aghalokpe, 28 September–2 October, 1988*

[1]*kpekere*   fried or roasted, sliced unripe plantain
[2]*dodo*   fried, sliced ripe plantain
[3]*garri*   staple West African food made from cassava
[4]*Onoharigho*   an Okpara man who brought rubber seeds from Burma
after the Second World War
[5]*Odjoboro*   a man in Urhobo mythology. Built a boat with cheap wood
which was wrecked in a turbulent storm
[6]*akata*   slim, tough and supple plant
[7]*oware*   freshwater fish of the Niger Delta
[8]*ovworo*   big, rather flat, fish of the Niger Delta

# On the Fourth Anniversary

*for my father*

I
I took a longer time
to grow
than others – after all,
I wasn't going to rear a hen
that would grow teeth
in my lifetime.
I had to fight
through every peril
the passage holds
to secure rights.
A hard lot is not
a disadvantaged fort.
I fly mad kites
over the blood-lit zone
of falcons.
Why did I fear
*Okrobogbowovo*[1], that ogre
that blazed a cold trail
in desolate paths?
Perhaps I needed the chill
of adolescence
to heat up
into a spirited man.
May the seasons fortify me
and enhance my prayer
to sleep without nightmares
and wake into suns of grace.

II
Since you left,
I have been repainting you
in my closet
with brighter and smoother colours.
I see fresh facets, invisible
in your lifetime.
With your two hands
you placed on my head
a fortune.
Who else but only you
could be the vessel
of this proud name?
It's the fourth anniversary
of your return
and my heart weeps
incessant streams, more
than when a courier letter
broke the dream-run
and so expected news
of your demise.
Today you are more my father
and I am more your son
than when you were around.
And your praise-name I invoke
in every gathering
is token tribute
to your generous hands.

*24 November, 1988*

[1]*Okrobogbowovo*    a scaring ogre in Urhobo mythology

# Roads

There's no morsel
in the scented trail of the wolf,
having learnt to swallow
without a bite.
I must give up flowers
to deflate lust
for a wider vision.

Bullets have grazed my heart;
I have paid my toll
through the road of passion
to see the end, the heart's worth
on a stone slab . . .

I have answered my praise-name
with a silent nod
in the company of hunters,
gone to harvest virtues
of seasoned days
with blistered hands
but without a tear.

I have paid the toll
to know the true worth
of passing through a sparse road.
I am the slave
thrown a cowrie by his master;
with it I perform the ritual
of freedom.
I fly through the eye
of a black storm;
with thunderbolt for a sling,
let me strike
at the tribe of rabid dogs;
let me leave behind
flares of total rout.

And when next I come across
the beast in its den,
I will smother fear
with ritual flares
and maul the villain
with the secret chant of my guts.
The road to freedom is always there
but strewn with snares.

# I Rejoice in the Rain

Rain raises my desire
with fresh memories of landmarks
beyond mountains of clouds;
rain fills me
with choral music of the cosmos.
What will flower
without a flush of wetness?

Rain is tears
held back
when the sun ignites the day
with missiles of smiles;
rain accelerates currents
to parched tongues —
remember how we wilted
in the sordid season
of sun-worship.

Rain dilutes the hemlock
of deceit, state charity,
with generous god-brewed doses.
Before now, there was
no dew every dawn
to wipe expectant faces
for a flood of vision.

When rain soaks the tear-
blind and sweat-sogged,
the face is lit
with liberty.
It rains loud
in the grove of faith,
rains streams of years
with remembrances of watermarks,
rains abundance of crops.
There's no sunstroke
underwater.

Now we can irrigate the land
into fields of industry
where fruits are fleshed
with native salt.
I rejoice in the rain,
transfused with divine draughts.

# Seascape

The sea green cascades into sand
with a white flush.
The spray smacks the lips
with salt and fish flavour.
Riot of waters, receding ripples,
multiple somersaults,
a shifting range,
a crash,
and smashed calm.

The charging spirit unleashes
the lioness from the deeps,
spreads her manes,
spends its own breath
for a breeze of cool fans.
To the skyline an eternity.

I leave my taints
to the sea,
leave with a heart
deeper than the sea-bed,
fighting, falling
and rising with strength.

# THE
# WARRIOR'S
# TRAIL

# Witnesses

These marks are not tattoos that
beauticians impressed upon the land's face;
they are scars that carry sharp pain.
We blame ourselves for all the facts
that threw an opulent blindfold around us
and made us slip into a big hole.
Eagles bartered their unassailable height
for draughts of an exotic weed-spiced mirage;
now sand-ridden, they reel from shortsightedness.
No mountain grows bigger the more it's quarried;
from the beginning we headed for debts.
Everybody sees the dark ahead.

# A Call

In palaces of chieftains
and shacks of tribesmen,
in every cardinal point
of the dispirited land,
the ivory horn shakes us
from our languid ears:
    let no one forget himself
    in the blindfold of clouds.

True, a dark sea
to weep days and years
but let no one drown
in the blind depth.
True, a nightscape
of monstrous haunts
but remember the eclipse's
a light recess.

Flywhisk dust off the body;
dispose of sackcloth, or
sew it into psychedelic robes —
there's a dance ahead
in the sun, naked delight
of faces lit with make-up.

Raze off the locks
that ache the head.
If the boat cannot sink
beneath the riverbed,
pain must exhaust its trials
to fortify us.

We wouldn't be abandoned
to cobweb corners,
we wouldn't seek
wilderness portions.
We must carry ourselves
to the sun ahead

as the ivory horn shakes us
from our languid ears.

# Of Appointees and Swearing-ins

No swearing-in cleanses the appointee.

General prescription for all
reared wild on forbidden virtues:
'To the mountain, to the mountain.'
There in the sky the spring whose waters
annul the flash of Miss Naira, who has
millions to boast of she downed flat.

So that their odour of the stable
will not drowse the nation,
let the rank-scented cabinet
go to the mountain
whose peaked skull the sun pats.

There, no hand-wash alone,
no face-wash alone;
they must stand naked before the world
below the downpour, cold in its mysteries;
they must stand upright with outstretched hands
intoning the Oath of Lightning's Blade
to smite the deviant . . .

The big seat's not meant for those
who are too comfortable to ascend the rocks,
not for pigs for whom a bath's no use,
not for those who carry some other rocks
in their heads – enough task to wrestle with –
not for those who trade off the flag for fortification
or the eagle mascot for foreign exchange.

All who wear the livery of state,
to the nipple of the mother rock
to suckle clear waters of truth.
The prayers at the fountain-head
take on wings on the lip,
and so to the mountain spring
herd the flock, herd the flock

for no swearing-in cleanses the appointee.

# Annals of the Tribe

Their hearts sunk into unknown depths,
how can they retrieve their heights?
They wailed and wailed to themselves;
they flaunted empty spaces
where hearts had stood as powerhouses –
they have lost the fire and the hearth.
They wailed and wailed to themselves;
behind them trails of losses:
they have lost the salt streams and mountains,
they have lost their gods and shadows.
Their wails rebounced upon their ears,
they feared the omen of tireless tears
but had forgotten how to dam the salt floods
that overpowered them young and old
and made a mess of their praise-names.
How could they see their hearts
with cataract eyes, how could
they take in the message of grace
with their scurvy ears,
how could they move forward
with limbs atrophied from
mistrust of a forward thrust?
They wailed and wailed to themselves
the only knowledge they had in abundance;
they sat upon their losses
and loved the marks of their memory.
They did not love themselves,
they lost their hearts,
they lost their heights,
they lost their fire and hearth,
they lost their salt,
they lost their streams and mountains,
they lost their gods and shadows,

they lost their eyes and ears,
they lost their limbs,
they lost their praise-names,
they lost themselves.
They wailed and wailed to themselves
because they loved losses
and what's sunk into unknown depths
is gone for frightened faces!

## On the Line

Laughter folded its toothsome spread
and left the land to its moody face,
prosperity forbade them on threat of death
from touching the hem of its robes,
love ruled out contact with them
since those who knocked heads together didn't know love.

In the scarcities that followed,
those who unearthed the gift of the tortoise
traded off the peace of the world to fill themselves,
those who still found a slice of earth to stand upon
dug holes with their toes to push neighbours into.

The seasons developed strange habits:
the days walked on their block heads
and dreams paraded phantoms of loved ones.
Years were crippled by falling standards
and they gave in to tearful floods.
Bats signed in as lords of new estates
and built their palaces in the dark.
Every face wrinkled to the wild sun
that had exhausted its tender strokes.

But breath remained like every other thing,
fractured and feeble, on a thin line.

# In Search of Heroes

No two of its kind in one neighbourhood,
the *akpobrisi*[1] tree surrounds itself with weeds.

The throne seats only one
and any feat or trick that blinds the public
exalts any of the aspirants to the mountain.

Behold the lurid battle of princes
at the funeral of their father!

Keep on your line,
a million pretenders in the wings
to break the long line
and pioneer a new rule.

Fanfare for the robed victor,
thrill of triumph in the ascent –
there's the crest of government
to lean upon in the palace.

We set out in old Benin
for the true prince,
and the usurper's shining sword
couldn't cut off the path of history.

After suffering nightmares of executions,
we picked him from a hide-out . . .
And that's why we persist.

With its bats night advances against us
and we must dig our feet into light.

[1] *akpobrisi*  a rare species of tree

# The Warrior's Trail

Ahead are barricades
with 'No Road' signs.
But the forbidden world knows
that over monstrous clouds
fruits of fortune.

Not everybody takes paths
beaten by others;
the lone one clears his own trail
for others to surge through
from the hyena's haunt
to freedom's open arms.

O Rabbit to whom darkness is pep,
I burrow with your teeth
through land plotted with perils.
And Spider, thread-spilling magician,
to your linkage craft
to speed me over holes . . .

# The Enormity of Sacrifice

When the messengers return, reduced
by perils of exploration
and speaking with split tongues,
we will have to grapple straight
with the enormity of sacrifice.
Can a proud bead pass through the nose
of the beast of offering?
What fire can we start in the forest
to blaze dead woods and demons
that halt the race?
What forked road can we build in the moon
to bring our dream wealth to dawn?
And in days with eroded memories
of family and friends, without knowledge
of tenderness in the veins,
hunters of the season will throw themselves
with gut slings ahead of them
into the open face of the buffalo of woes.
In the heat of combat, clouds of dust
and the enormity of sacrifice stares:
the land scarred beyond recognition,
body smudged with blood and sweat,
the face scary with contortions.
When dust has settled upon the day,
bruised hands will plant new trees
that will grow on the tear-sodden soil,
trees to tether our totem bull.

# Summoning Men and Gods

Now we must battle-dress ourselves
to attack the scurrilous scab
that blacks out the land's beauty
and warps the womb into a dry sack

now we must throw back the bribes
of Order of the Niger and National Merit Award
at murderers and their bloody hands
and haunt them to death with memory-
filled shafts of conscience

now we must aim straight shots
at the capital coven of the day,
the island den of robbers;
now we must break the rock of patience –
Lagos and Abuja must become the graveyards
of werewolves of state

now we must summon gut-filled gods
from their raw abodes in the astral wilderness
to smite demigods of stolen cash,
arch-constrictors of hope;
now we must only invoke terrible gods
to power the veins into the field

now we must assemble an all-time army
to smash the affront of beauty
by the soldiery of slavish salutes;
now we must say goodbye to the haven
of silence and acquiescence where we shut ourselves

now we must fortify ourselves
with the howls of victims we have to rescue
from the strangle-hold of the hydra-heads,
now we must say goodbye to fear
and break new grounds with our warsongs

now we must wield iron and exhale fire . . .

# Pains

This labour for all its bite
must be borne without groans.
Let it not be told
that Mother lacked the grit
of a lioness to deliver and so
defiled the good luck of our guest
with uncontrolled tears.
As she fast descends the mountain,
three months a monster of the tribe,
let it not be told
that Mother couldn't absorb
the dastard kicks of a torturer-friend
and gave up rather than relieve
her children of lifetimes of pain.
Even trees bear the tyranny of seasons,
the neem is my rugged witness;
even small animals raise their heads
in front of fox fires,
the ant is queen in the daemon world.
And gently, gently, without a howl
the fowl lays eggs.
We have learnt not to complain of bitterness
after consuming the rat to the tail!
With the brunt of the mountain
achieved in morning sickness
and gasping nights of sweat,
with the vision of a baby
talking from the womb
and growing upper teeth first,
this labour for all its bite
must be borne without groans.

# You Know Why

*for Felie*

We must hum these notes to ourselves,
absorb their fragrance into the vein
to bloom radiance in the face.

I had sung of stars
and thought it was all I could praise.
I had not come to the song of songs.

You are the promised vision,
incandescent flower of light;
you outshine diamonds.

With your light I comb cosmic lanes
for undiscovered jewels;
nobody will be richer than me.

For you I know no bounds,
for you my days long for dreams,
I am drunk in our flight of wonder birds:

      the moon is ours to keep
          the shield is ours to hold
              the war is ours to win.

In another place I would give you flowers.
Here we have lit a bonfire in the heart
to celebrate gains of exploration.

I know how to sing with naked words
but not to sell this prized world
to the cheap eyes of the public

we must hum these notes to ourselves,
absorb their fragrance into the vein
to bloom radiance in the face.

# *Full Moon*

Full to the very brim of night,
the moon displays her light-rated body
with a bevy of legendary beauty aids.
With her incandescent disc of white,
she transports her congregation
to break faithless habits of gloom:
the lame to procure wings with light,
the poor to possess wealth of light,
the weak to gain strength from the gaiety of light.

And you are full moon in my life:
in your generous luminance I build
a pyramid of love with pygmy hands.

# Cross-country

Look through my genes for the trademark of wolves,
you who still cannot separate me from a rapacious pack.

Must every tree-branch turn crooked in the wind,
must every season wear dust on its leaf-drawn face?

Am I limbed with diabolical daggers of claws
that can tear off others' portions to overfill mine?

Must I be lynched in the heat of the Sahel
for squandering floods of rain across the delta?

If the moon cannot pick out her mad lover
from the hordes of gamesters, pity the heart.

And if this song cannot drown regional drums of
                                        suspicion,
the cross-country love falters before fruition.

Do you look through my genes for the trademark of
                                        wolves,
you who still cannot separate me from the rapacious tribe?

# Essi's Matchet

The drums of Agbassa grove,
a full traffic after silent decades,
bring Essi back to life.
With ritual steps the warrior's
matchet clears a way
through unending tangles.

There are goals behind tall bushes;
with arm-swishes of sharp blows
we come over monstrous cover —
fruits flash ripe colours,
and the secret's sold out
to be sowed in the head . . .

The walls of our defences
rise to the sky;
our missiles carry the fire
of the lightning god —
we have acquired the spirit
of the lion in whose haunt
we were born.

We foreswear the anthem
of faithless days; no longer
sing after prodigal voices
*whatever their might
the soldiering ants
cannot cart away an egg
from their forays.*
Power's not always seen
in its naked armour.

With the vision of the victor,
we shake off the succubus
to breathe freely;
before the eyes of the lion,
we rise beyond ourselves
to wield Essi's matchet
of right and might.

# Kwanza[1]

## I

The first fruits of the tedious season
blossom beyond the pale of public eyes.
The wind, excited from a spiced carriage,
blows the fruitful tidings with zest.
The savour already fills the palate
with draughts of unprecedented smiles.
Each day adds more gold to the robes
that the land sweated to procure from industry;
each vision is filled with fields of fertility.
Though the yield cannot yet be measured,
the grim army of famine that unleashed sadism
already turns its back and flees;
the bruised land breaks its skeletal mould
into a hand-groomed idol of a hundred million.

## II

Those who mocked our naked hands for lack of industry
will be ashamed of their ignorance of palmistry,
those who jeered at our play-punctuated warsongs as idle
songs
will join us in the proud anthem of survival,
those who saw our bonfire as a conflagration of kinsmen
will witness the blood bond of our brotherhood outlive
hearsays,
those who saw a landscape riddled with bones of pain
will see the transience of hopeful tears,
those who saw death in the assault of monsters
will clap for the good luck of small ones.
In our time the patient sun tunnels
through mountain clouds and a vast obsidian night
into the fresh radiance of a cheerful dawn.

[1]*Kwanza*   in Kiswahili means the first fruit

# No Longer

No longer is the tiger roaming the jungle
blazing a desolate trail.
We couldn't talk or laugh.

We caught him in his rare sleep –
if not then, who dares
break into the den?

Now that he is tamed,
that light once dissipated in revelries
will shine into every home.

We thrust out arms
eyes burning like logfire
and the tiger cast off murderous habit
from his blood.

The land is so beautiful
when breathing free.

# The Power to Overpower

Without the iron suit of the mahogany tree,
the saw wouldn't grow teeth of steel —
conquest demands power to overpower.

Without blood-thirsty rites of tyranny,
the weak wouldn't invoke their guts —
the sight of death gives wings to the lame.

Without the night-dominating practice of witches,
the lords of the land wouldn't know fear —
there's no security in any height.

Without the guerrilla blows of death,
life wouldn't be so precious —
the confidence of gods breeds cheap arrogance.

And so we need waves to shark our way through life,
need a long road to sharpen the soles,
need a sky of a mountain to grow wings.

# Epilogue: Spoken by the Chorus

We have cut the cobra's tail
and rejoice at striking a death blow,
but the enemy already throws its head loose
and the land will not rest.
We shower tears to celebrate or grieve:
we can only ask for more of the salt of smiles
and not for none of that of agonising pain.
We have shed blood for peace,
had love savaged by beastly wiles.
Perhaps we cannot come out as total victors,
we win mock battles to swell our heads.
When a flash storm gathers tyrannical strength,
it breaks the only tall palm of the land.
Politics and the military are breeding grounds
for a summit of torturers.
We have cut the cobra's tail
but already the enemy throws its head loose
and the land has no rest from raids.
May it not re-appear with a more poisonous tail!